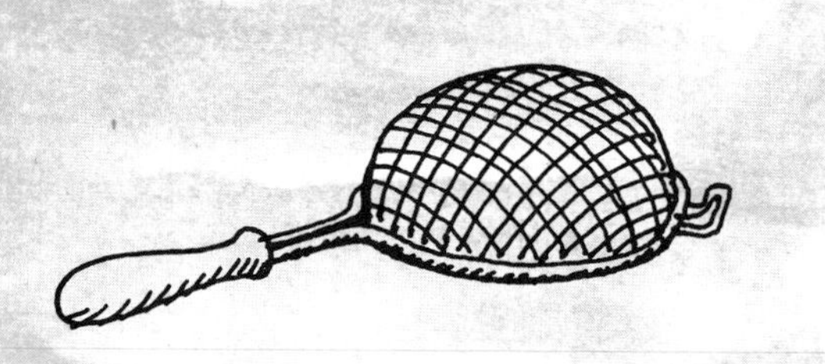

A STRAINER..for draining, and for washing fruit-- like berries.

MEASURING CUPS... for exact measuring.

A BUTTER KNIFE... for spreading butter, mayonnaise, cheese, and other mixtures.

A PITCHER... for punch, fruit drinks, and other beverages.

A MIXING BOWL... in which to whip cream, and mix ingredients.

A ROTARY BEATER... for whipping cream.

A JUICER... for squeezing juice from oranges and lemons.

A SALAD BOWL... in which to prepare, present, and toss salads.

# THE A to Z NO-COOK COOKBOOK

BY FELIPE ROJAS-LOMBARDI
ILLUSTRATED BY DOROTHY IVENS

PORTRAIT OF FELIPE ROJAS-LOMBARDI
ON THE BACK COVER OF THE BOOK
BY NORMAN ROCKWELL

PUBLISHED BY R-L CREATIONS INC. NEW YORK
2 WEST 45th. STREET, NEW YORK, N.Y. 10036
DISTRIBUTED by WORLD PUBLISHING COMPANY

COPYRIGHT © 1972 BY R-L CREATIONS, INC.
ALL RIGHTS RESERVED
LIBRARY OF CONGRESS CATALOG CARD NUMBER 72-79753

PRINTED IN THE UNITED STATES OF AMERICA
BY METROPOLITAN PRINTING CO.
PORTLAND, OREGON

FELIPE ROJAS-LOMBARDI *2 West 45 Street, New York, N.Y. 10036*

Dear Friend,

How would you like to have a real adventure, right at home? There are all kinds of adventures, but cooking is one of the best. It is also fun. This adventure will take place in your own kitchen, and before long you'll be making all kinds of sandwiches, drinks, and lots of other food you'll love to eat, and have your family and friends share with you. First of all, we want our parents to feel comfortable when we have our cooking adventures. They will be glad to know we don't have to work with sharp knives, boiling water, flames, or use any utensils that could be harmful, even to grownups. Of course, we must always be careful when we are working in the kitchen. Cleanliness is very important. Let us begin with clean hands, and the food we handle must be clean. After all, we will be eating the food we touch. Don't forget to leave the kitchen clean; this is the place where we keep our food.

Just between us, I made lots of mistakes when I was a child learning to cook. You may not have a dish prepared right the first time, but don't be discouraged. You'll learn to do it right. I have never forgotten how happy and proud I was when I learned how to prepare my first dish. It was a sandwich, and I made it when I was five years old. It was great fun then and it is still fun. I hope you have as much fun in the kitchen as I do. Please write and let me know how YOU are enjoying your cooking adventures. I promise to answer your letter!

Your friend,

Felipe

F. Rojas-Lombardi

# APPETIZER

YOU NEED:

watercress
8 carrot sticks
8 celery sticks
8 radishes, cut in half
8 scallions
8 cherry tomatoes
½ cup mayonnaise
2 tablespoons sour cream
¼ cup Blue cheese

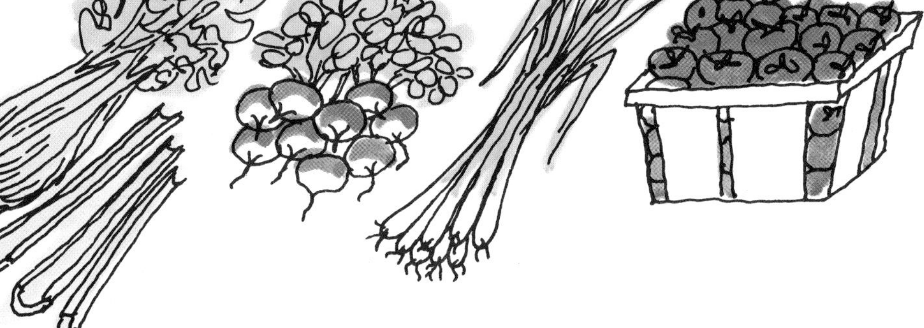

WHAT YOU DO:

1. Spread the watercress over a serving plate.
2. Arrange carrot sticks, celery sticks, radishes, scallions and cherry tomatoes on top of the watercress.
3. In a cereal bowl, mash the Blue cheese with a fork.
4. Put the mayonnaise and sour cream in with the Blue cheese and mix them all together.
5. Put the mixture in a cup and place the cup in the center of the serving plate.

# APPLE SALAD

YOU NEED:

1 sliced apple
1 sliced celery
3 walnuts, cut in small pieces
1 teaspoon raisins
2 tablespoons shredded Swiss or American cheese
2 tablespoons mayonnaise
salt and pepper
2 lettuce leaves

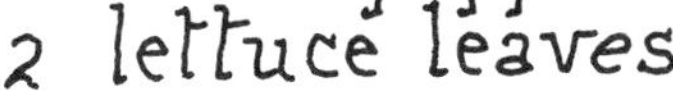

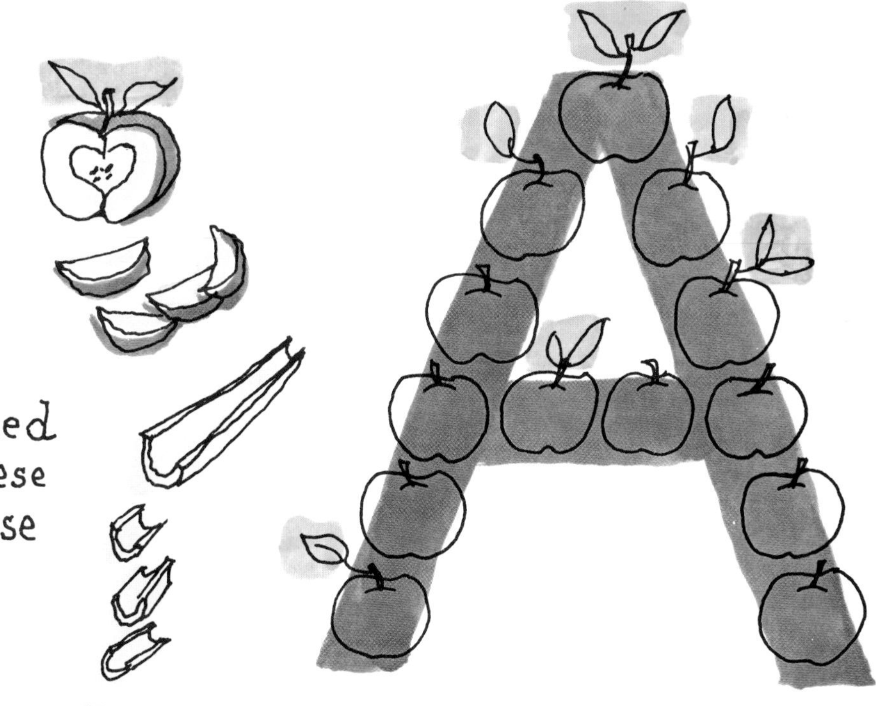

WHAT YOU DO:

1. In a cereal bowl, mix the apples, celery, walnuts, raisins and cheese.
2. Put the mayonnaise into the mixture.
3. Carefully add a little salt and pepper to taste.
4. Divide into two portions and place each portion on a lettuce leaf, on salad plates.

# BANANA SOUTH SEAS

YOU NEED:

1 banana
1 tablespoon shredded coconut
2 tablespoons milk
1 tablespoon honey
a little cinnamon

WHAT YOU DO:

1. Peel and slice the banana.
2. Place the sliced banana on a soup plate.
3. Sprinkle the banana with the shredded coconut.
4. Pour the milk over the banana.
5. Pour honey over the banana.
6. Sprinkle a little cinnamon on top of the honey.

If you do not have coconut, you may use other kinds of nuts, cut into tiny pieces.

# BERRIES AND CREAM

YOU NEED:

- ½ cup heavy cream
- 1 tablespoon confectioners sugar
- ⅛ teaspoon orange extract (you may use vanilla extract instead)
- 1 cup of your favorite berries, (strawberries, blackberries, blueberries, etc.)

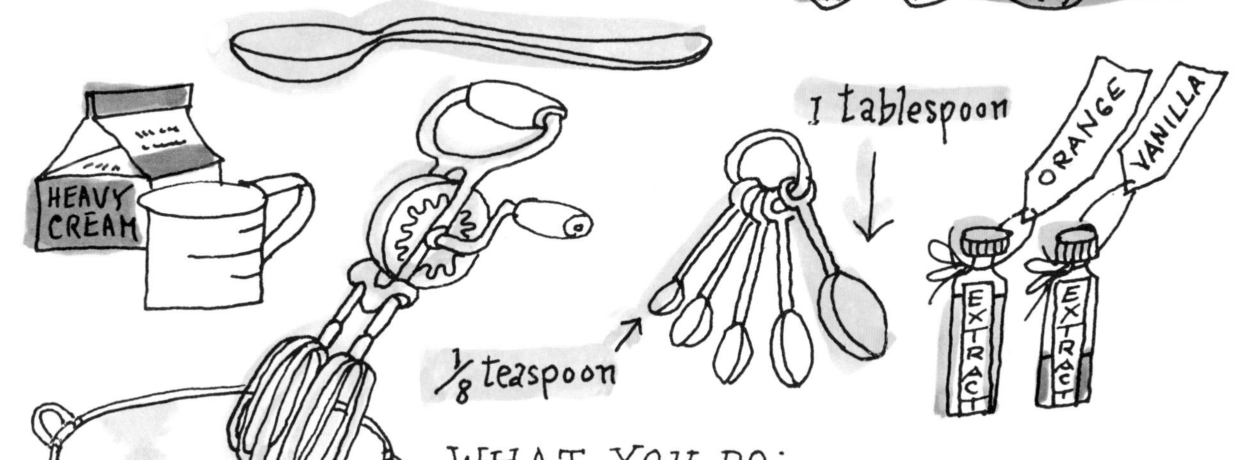

WHAT YOU DO:

1. Put the heavy cream, sugar and extract into the mixing bowl. Beat with a rotary beater until thick.
2. If the mixture doesn't get as thick as you may like it, add another tablespoon of sugar and beat some more.
3. Pick off all the stems from the berries, then rinse and drain the berries.
4. Stir the berries into the cream gently and serve.

**If you want to make this really fancy, sprinkle some chopped walnuts on top.**

# COLD CEREAL DELIGHT

YOU NEED:

½ bowl of your favorite cereal
1 scoop vanilla ice cream
1 sliced peach or 1 sliced banana
¼ cup of cold milk
1 spoonful of preserves

WHAT YOU DO:

1. Place ½ a bowl of your favorite cereal in a cereal bowl.
2. Place a scoop of vanilla ice cream on top of the cereal.
3. Place some canned or fresh fruit such as peach or banana on top of the cereal, and pour ¼ cup of cold milk over it.
4. Put a spoonful of your favorite preserve over the ice cream.

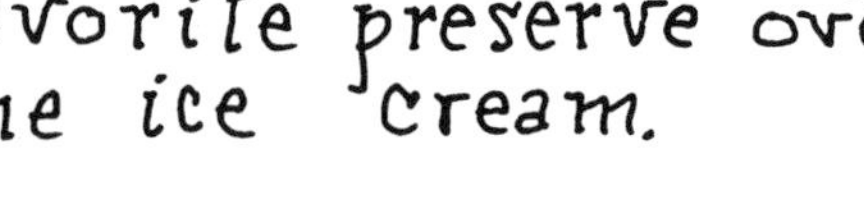

# CREAMY CARROT BITS

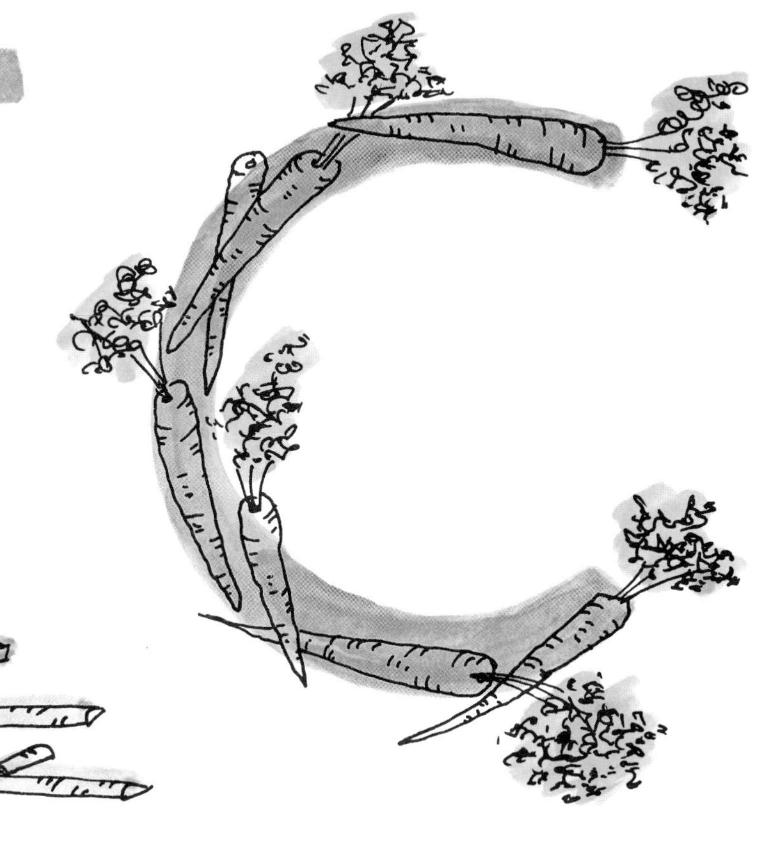

YOU NEED:

2 thin carrots
3 ounces cream cheese
1 tablespoon sour cream
salt and pepper
1/4 teaspoon of dried dill, or
1 teaspoon of cut fresh dill

WHAT YOU DO:

1. Cut 2 thin carrots in slices after you have washed and peeled them.
2. Put the cream cheese in a cereal bowl.
3. Soften the cheese with a fork.
4. Put the sour cream in with the cheese, and add a tiny bit of salt and pepper.
5. Mix all this together with a spoon.
6. Place the carrot slices on a plate.
7. Spread the cream cheese mixture over the carrots.
8. Eat the carrots with your fingers.
9. Sprinkle dill on the cream cheese mixture.

If you would like to do what the chefs do, put the carrots on a bed of parsley.

# DINNER SANDWICH

YOU NEED:

- 3 slices of white bread, toasted if you like
- mayonnaise
- 2 slices of ham
- 2 slices of tomato
- 1 tablespoon of cut up onions
- 2 slices of American cheese
- 1 lettuce leaf

WHAT YOU DO:

1. Spread mayonnaise over one slice of bread.
2. Place 2 slices of ham on the slice of bread.
3. Place 2 slices of tomato on top of the ham.
4. Sprinkle tomatoes with the cut pieces of onion.
5. Spread mayonnaise on both sides of the second slice of bread.
6. Place the second slice of bread on top of the ham and tomatoes. Sprinkle with a tiny bit of salt and pepper.
7. Place 2 slices of American cheese on top of the second slice of bread.
8. Cover the cheese with lettuce leaf.
9. Spread some mayonnaise on one side of third slice of bread and place it on top of the cheese and lettuce.

You now have a real mouth-stuffer sandwich that tastes great with a glass of milk. You can serve this with an olive or a piece of pickle.

# DOUGHNUT YUMMY

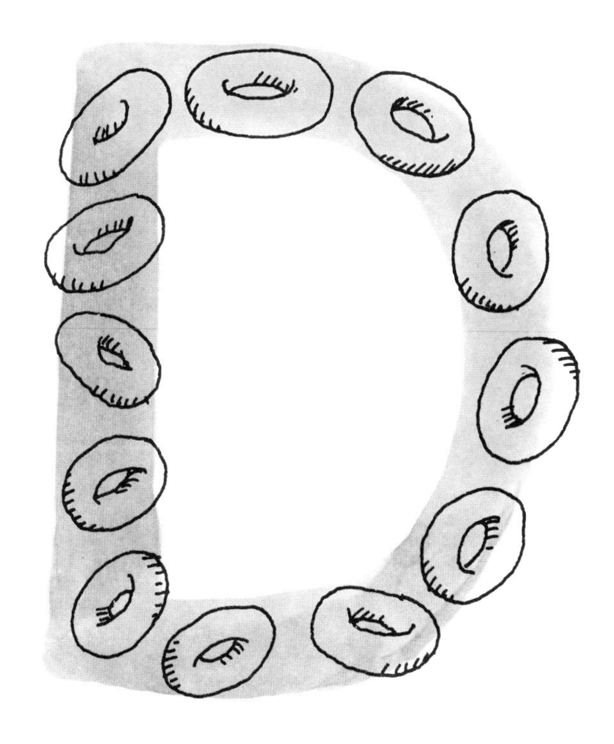

YOU NEED:

- 1 doughnut
- 1 scoop of ice cream
- 1 tablespoon chopped nuts
- 1 teaspoon confectioners sugar

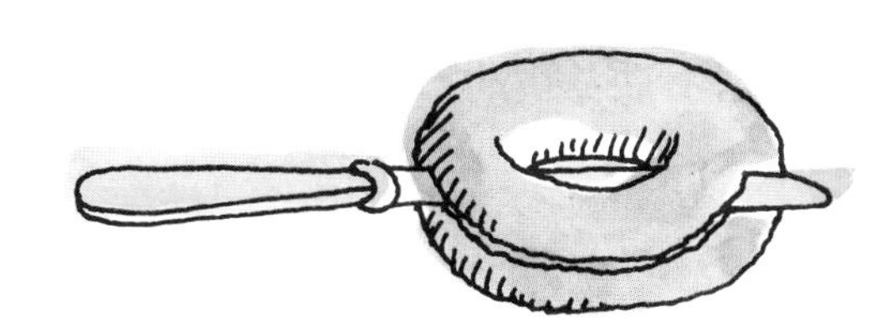

WHAT YOU DO:

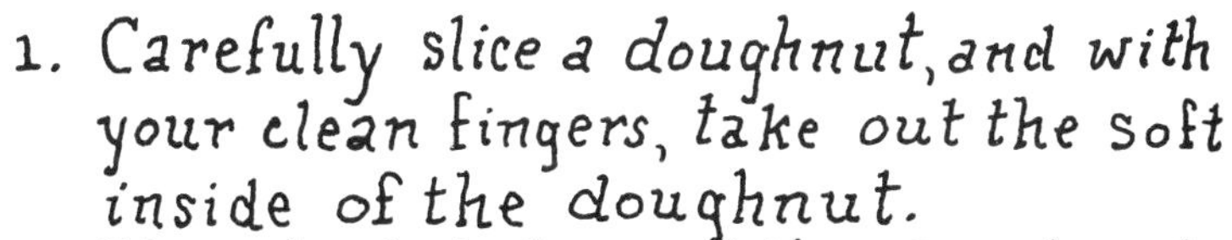

1. Carefully slice a doughnut, and with your clean fingers, take out the soft inside of the doughnut.
2. Place both halves of the doughnut on a plate.
3. In a cereal bowl, put a scoop of your favorite ice cream, and soften it with a fork.
4. Put the chopped nuts in with the ice cream and mix them together.
5. With a spoon, fill the doughnut with ice cream.
6. Put both sides of the doughnut together like a sandwich.
7. Sprinkle the top with the confectioners sugar.

# EGG PUNCH

## YOU NEED

- 1 large raw egg
- 2 tablespoons honey
- 1/4 teaspoon vanilla extract
- a tiny bit of salt
- a tiny bit of nutmeg (optional)
- 1 cup milk

## WHAT YOU DO:

1. In the mixing bowl, break open the egg.
2. Put the honey, vanilla extract, salt and nutmeg in with the egg.
3. Shake everything together in the tightly covered jar until it is all mixed.
4. Pour the milk into the egg mixture and shake again until it is all well mixed.
5. If you like it cold, put it in the refrigerator for one hour.

The Egg Punch is delicious served with cookies.

# ENGLISH MUFFIN SNACK

YOU NEED:

1 English muffin
butter
cream cheese
jelly

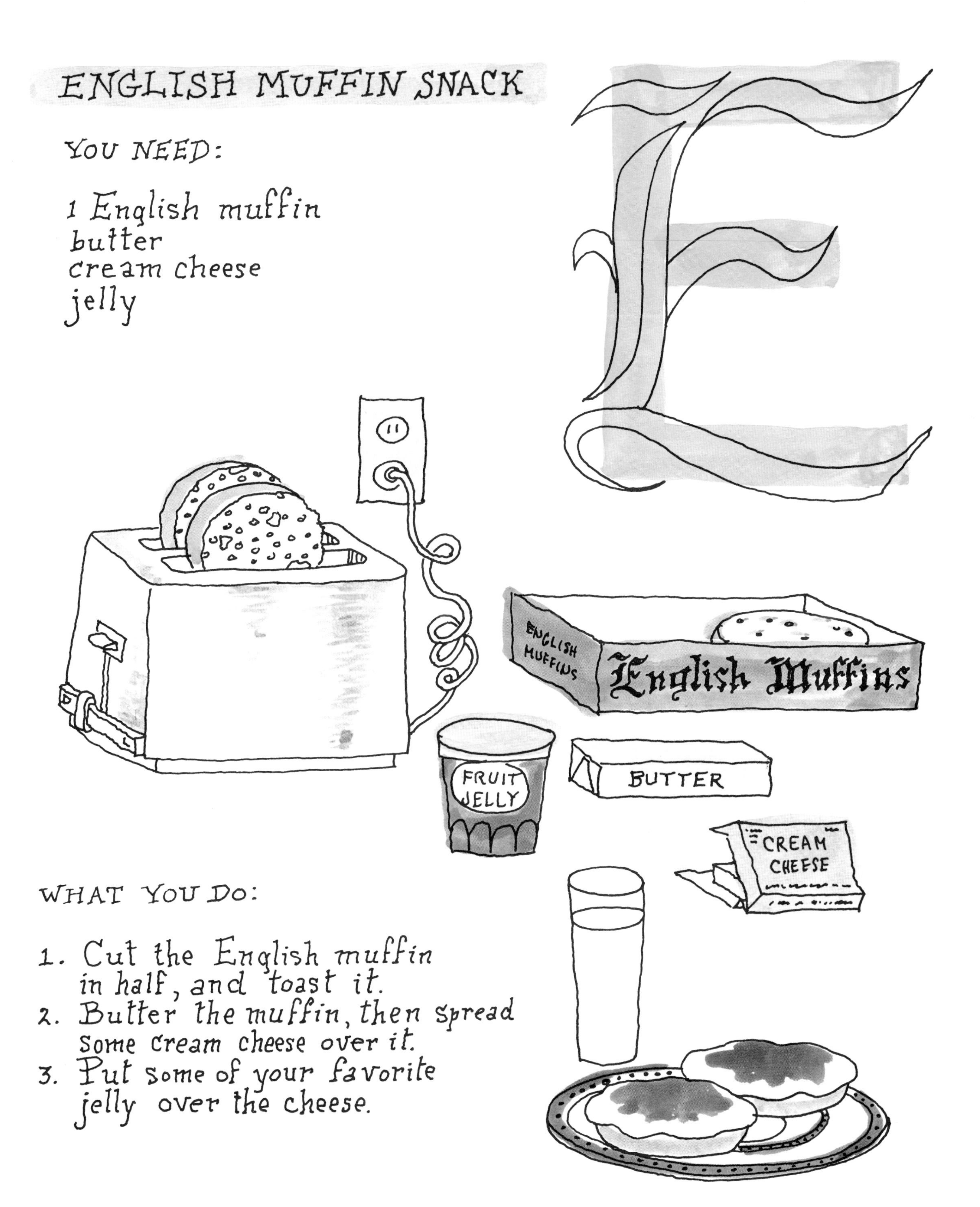


WHAT YOU DO:

1. Cut the English muffin in half, and toast it.
2. Butter the muffin, then spread some cream cheese over it.
3. Put some of your favorite jelly over the cheese.

# FROZEN PEANUT BUTTER TREAT

YOU NEED:

½ pint sour cream
½ cup peanut butter with chunks
½ cup granulated sugar
2 tablespoons grape jelly

WHAT YOU DO:

1. In a metal mixing bowl, put the sour cream, peanut butter and sugar, and mix very well.
2. Place the mixture in the freezer section of the refrigerator for 24 hours.
3. To serve, scoop out onto plates and put grape jelly on top.

# FRUIT SALAD

YOU NEED:

¼ cup of grapes, cut in half
1 pear, quartered, core removed
1 orange, peeled and separated into segments.
1 small can pineapple chunks, drained
2 tablespoons mayonnaise
1 teaspoon sour cream
2 large lettuce leaves
2 tablespoons chopped walnuts
2 Maraschino cherries

WHAT YOU DO:

1. Mix the grapes, pear, orange and pineapple all together in a mixing bowl.
2. In a cereal bowl, mix the mayonnaise and sour cream.
3. Put the mayonnaise and sour cream in with the fruit and stir all together until fruit is coated.
4. Put a lettuce leaf on each salad plate.
5. Divide the fruit salad in half and place each half on a lettuce leaf.
6. Sprinkle some of the nuts over each salad portion, and top with a cherry.

# GARLIC BREAD

YOU NEED:

¼ stick of butter
1 clove of garlic, crushed
4 slices of bread

WHAT YOU DO:

1. Soften the butter with a fork.
2. Mash the garlic with a fork, so that you can mix it with the butter.
3. Mix the butter with the garlic.
4. Spread the mixture lightly over slices of bread.
5. Put slices of bread in the toaster.
6. When you take the bread out of the toaster, spread some more of the garlic butter on the toasted bread.

**This is good with soup.**

# GRAPEFRUIT GOODNESS

YOU NEED:

1 grapefruit
2 teaspoons sugar
a tiny sprinkle of cinnamon
2 Maraschino cherries

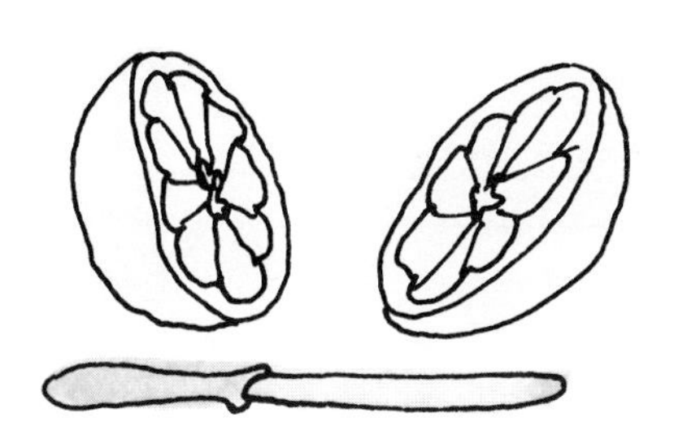

WHAT YOU DO:

1. Cut the grapefruit in half.
2. Sprinkle each half with a teaspoon of sugar, and a tiny sprinkle of cinnamon.
3. Put a Maraschino cherry in the center of each half.
4. Place grapefruit in the refrigerator to chill until ready to serve.

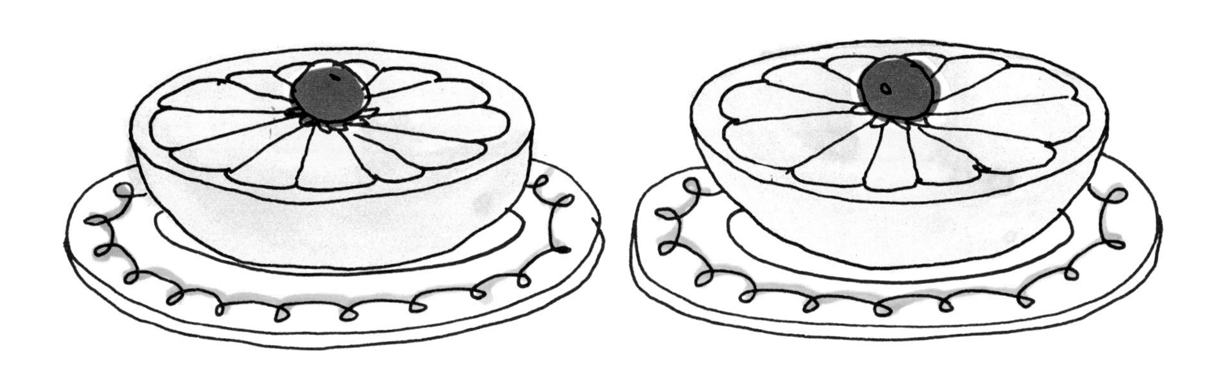

# HONEY BUTTER

YOU NEED:

¼ cup butter
4 tablespoons honey

WHAT YOU DO:

1. Soften the butter at room temperature, mash it with a fork.
2. Add the honey to the butter and mix well, until it makes a paste.

This is good for spreading on toast, or when Mother makes waffles, or to put on top of pancakes. Team up with your mother. She'll make the waffles and pancakes and you make the Honey Butter.

# HERO SANDWICH

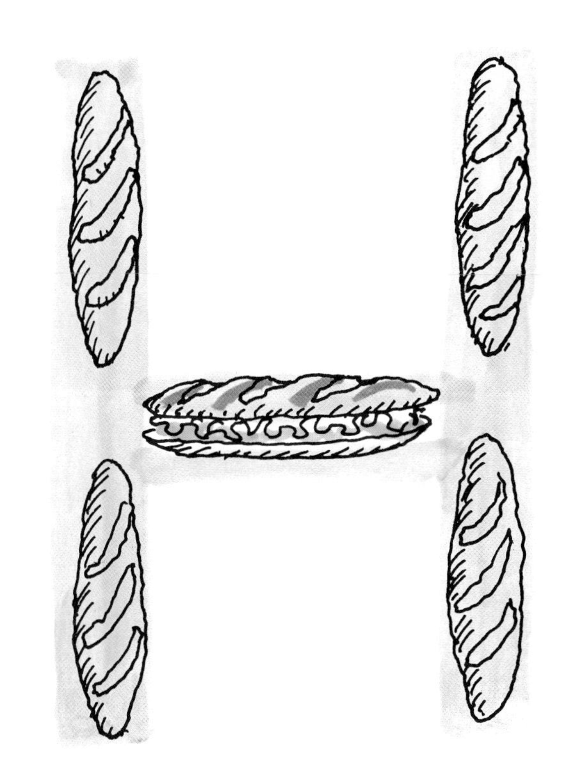

YOU NEED:

1 small hero bread, cut in half, lengthwise
butter
1 lettuce leaf
¼ teaspoon oil
½ teaspoon vinegar
1 tablespoon sliced pitted green olives
2 slices of tomato
salt, pepper, oregano
3 slices of ham
2 slices of Provolone cheese
3 slices of turkey

WHAT YOU DO:

1. Remove some of the soft part from the inside of the bread, then butter inside both pieces of bread.
2. Tear the lettuce into small pieces, on a plate.
3. In a cup, mix the oil and vinegar together, and sprinkle over the lettuce.
4. Place the lettuce on one piece of bread, together with the olives and tomatoes.
5. Sprinkle with a tiny bit of salt, pepper and oregano.
6. Place ham, cheese, and turkey on top of the olives and tomatoes.
7. Cover with the other half of the bread.

# ICE CREAM AND MELON

YOU NEED:

1 small honeydew melon
2 scoops of vanilla ice cream
1 small can of black cherries, drained

WHAT YOU DO:

1. Cut the melon in half and remove all the seeds.
2. Put a scoop of ice cream in each half of the melon.
3. Top with black cherries, and serve on dessert plates.

# ICE CREAM CAKE

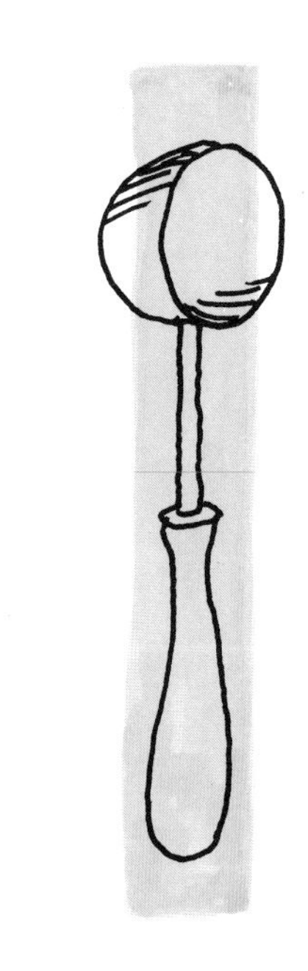

YOU NEED:

1 thin slice of your favorite cake
1 scoop of vanilla ice cream
1 scoop of chocolate ice cream
1 scoop of strawberry ice cream
1 small can peaches, drained
2 tablespoons strawberry or
  chocolate syrup
1 tablespoon chopped nuts

WHAT YOU DO:

1. Place a thin slice of cake on a salad plate.
2. Cover the cake with 3 scoops of ice cream.
3. Place the peaches all around the ice cream.
4. Pour the strawberry or chocolate syrup over the ice cream.
5. Garnish with chopped nuts.

# JAMANCHEESE SANDWICH

YOU NEED:

cream cheese
2 slices of fresh rye bread
your favorite jam

WHAT YOU DO:

1. Spread cream cheese over one slice of bread.
2. Top with some of your favorite jam.
3. Cover with second slice of bread.

This sandwich is good with milk or hot chocolate.

# JAPANESE SALAD

YOU NEED:

- 1/4 teaspoon vinegar
- 1/3 cup soy sauce
- 1/4 teaspoon of grated fresh ginger, or 1/2 teaspoon cut up crystallized ginger
- 1 large cucumber, sliced
- 1/2 cup of cooked shrimp

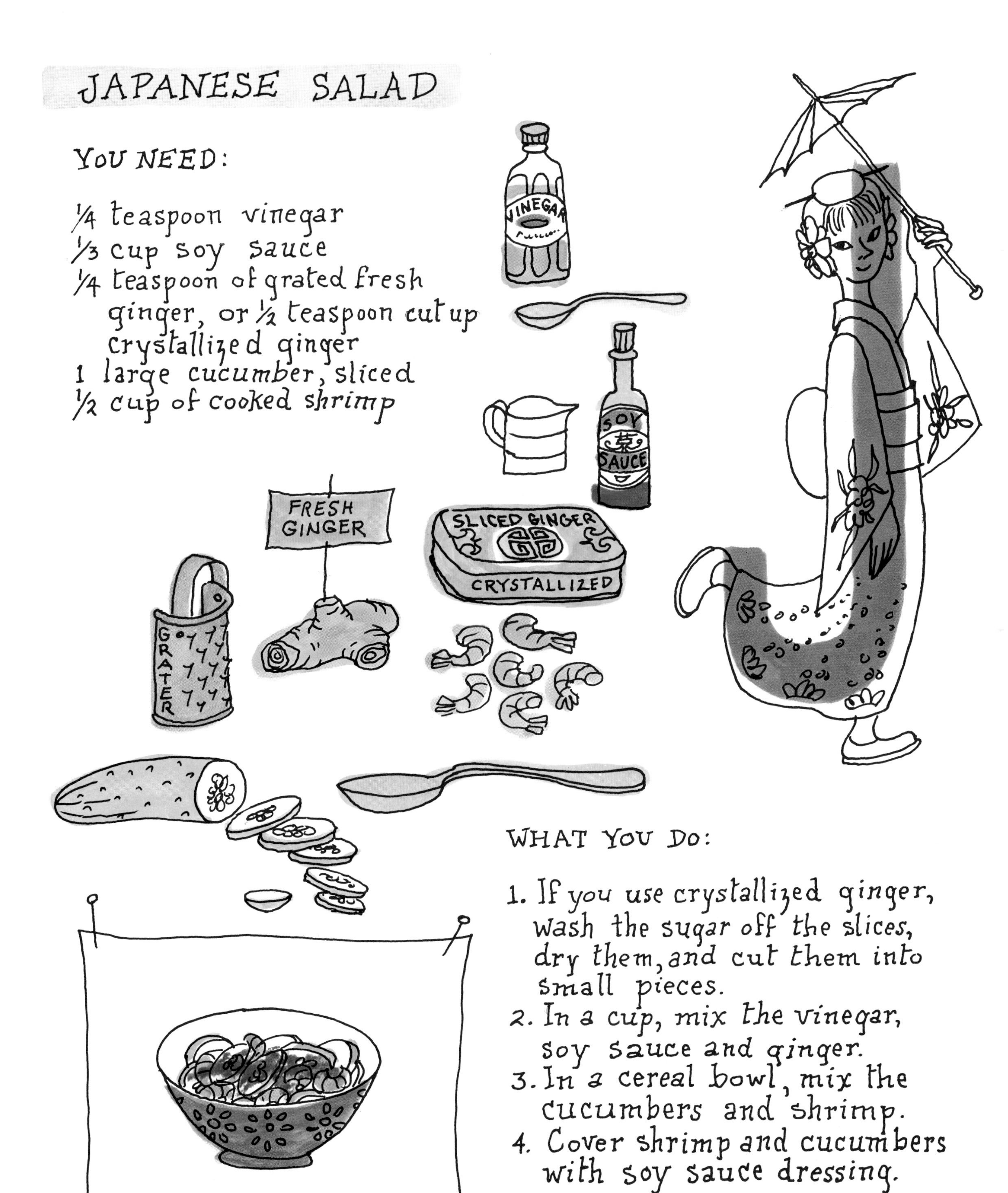


WHAT YOU DO:

1. If you use crystallized ginger, wash the sugar off the slices, dry them, and cut them into small pieces.
2. In a cup, mix the vinegar, soy sauce and ginger.
3. In a cereal bowl, mix the cucumbers and shrimp.
4. Cover shrimp and cucumbers with soy sauce dressing.

# KENTUCKY MINT JULEP JR.

YOU NEED:

1 can frozen lemonade concentrate
sugar to taste
1 sliced lemon
½ tray of ice cubes
1 cup of ginger ale
mint leaves

WHAT YOU DO:

1. Open can of lemonade concentrate and put it into a pitcher.
2. Add water as directed on the can.
3. Add sugar to taste, sliced lemon, ice cubes and ginger ale.
4. Stir well, until pitcher is frosted on the outside.
5. Garnish with mint leaves.

# KIDNEY BEAN SALAD

YOU NEED:

1 cup of canned kidney beans
1 tomato, cut in quarters
1 onion, sliced
1 tablespoon oil
1 teaspoon vinegar
2 lettuce leaves
salt and pepper
1 sprig of parsley, torn up

WHAT YOU DO:

1. Open and drain can of kidney beans.
2. Put cup of kidney beans in a salad bowl.
3. Mix beans with tomatoes and onions.
4. In a cup, mix the oil, vinegar and a tiny bit of salt and pepper.
5. Pour oil mixture over vegetables and mix all well together.
6. Take 2 salad plates and put a lettuce leaf on each one.
7. Divide kidney bean mixture in half, and place a portion on each lettuce leaf. Put the bits of parsley on top.

# LETTUCE SALAD

## YOU NEED:

1 small head of Boston or iceberg lettuce
4 spinach leaves
small bunch of watercress
½ cup mayonnaise
2 tablespoons Blue cheese
pepper to taste

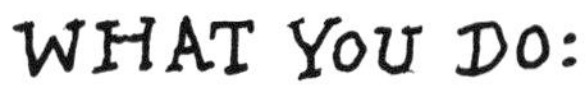

## WHAT YOU DO:

1. Wash and dry the vegetables.
2. Break up the lettuce into bite size pieces.
3. Take off the thick stems of the watercress. Use only the thin tender leaves.
4. Use the tender leaves of spinach.
5. Toss all the vegetables together in a salad bowl.
6. In a cup, mix the mayonnaise, Blue cheese, and a little pepper.
7. Place the mayonnaise mixture on top of the vegetables and mix together.

## LEFTOVER SANDWICH

YOU NEED:

2 slices of white bread
butter or mayonnaise
salt and pepper
lettuce leaf
leftover chicken, turkey or beef

WHAT YOU DO:

1. Toast the two slices of white bread.
2. Put butter or mayonnaise on one slice of the toast.
3. Place leftover chicken, turkey or beef on that piece of toast. Sprinkle with a little salt and pepper.
4. Place lettuce leaf over the chicken, turkey or beef, and cover with the other piece of toast.

Food must never be wasted, and leftovers can often be used for delicious snacks.

# MILK SHAKE

YOU NEED:

- 3/4 cup milk
- 1 scoop chocolate ice cream
- 1 tablespoon chocolate syrup

WHAT YOU DO:

1. Put milk, ice cream and chocolate syrup in a jar.
2. Put lid on jar tightly, and shake well until ice cream is melted and mixture is smooth.

To make a vanilla shake, use vanilla ice cream, and a drop of vanilla extract.

# MUSHROOMS AND LIMA BEANS

YOU NEED:

- 1 medium can of lima beans, drained
- 3 tablespoons of onions cut in tiny pieces.
- ½ pound mushrooms, sliced
- 2 tablespoons of celery cut into thin slices.
- 2 tablespoons salad or vegetable oil
- 1 teaspoon vinegar
- salt and pepper

WHAT YOU DO:

1. Open can of lima beans and drain in a strainer.
2. Put the beans in a salad bowl with the onions and celery.
3. Wash the mushrooms in the strainer and slice them. Put half in salad bowl.
4. In a cup, mix the oil, vinegar and a little salt and pepper.
5. Pour oil mixture in with vegetables and mix all together.
6. Garnish with the rest of the mushrooms.

Garnish means to decorate the food to make it attractive. The garnish is good food too.

# NUT SANDWICH

YOU NEED:

3 ounces of cream cheese
1 tablespoon milk
3 tablespoons pecans (or walnuts), cut in small pieces
4 slices of white bread

WHAT YOU DO:

1. Soften the cream cheese with a fork, and mix with milk.
2. Put the pecans or walnuts in with the cream cheese and mash all together until the mixture is soft, creamy, and easy to spread.
3. Toast the bread and spread cheese mixture on each slice. Serve separately, or make into sandwiches.

This is another delicious snack with milk or cocoa.

# NUT COMPOTE

YOU NEED:

- 1/4 cup of walnuts cut in small pieces
- 3/4 cup of tangerine segments
- 3/4 cup of diced peaches, (fresh or canned)
- 1/4 cup of sliced banana
- sugar, if you like

WHAT YOU DO:

1. Put the walnuts, tangerine segments, peaches, and bananas in a cereal bowl, and mix all together. Add a little sugar if needed.

# OREGON SANDWICH

## YOU NEED:

1 slice of meat loaf
2 slices of bread, spread with butter or mayonnaise
2 slices of tomato
Chili Sauce to taste

## WHAT YOU DO:

1. Place meat loaf slice on one slice of bread which has been buttered or spread with mayonnaise.
2. Cover meat loaf with Chili Sauce.
3. Top with tomato slices.
4. Cover with the other slice of bread, spread with butter or mayonnaise.

Serve with pickle relish. The Oregon Sandwich is a favorite with the Oregon woodsmen.

# ORANGE PUNCH

YOU NEED:

1 quart orange juice
4 slices of apple
2 thin slices of lemon
4 strawberries, each cut in half
a little sugar
¼ tray of ice cubes

WHAT YOU DO:

1. In a pitcher, put the orange juice, apple and lemon slices, and strawberries.
2. Add a little sugar, and stir until it dissolves.
3. Add the ice cubes
4. Stir until pitcher is frosted.

# PARTY POPS

YOU NEED:

16 cubes of pineapple
orange juice
16 popsicle sticks

WHAT YOU DO:

1. Fill the ice tray dividers with orange juice.
2. Put a cube of pineapple in each divider, with the orange juice.
3. Place the tray in freezer compartment of the refrigerator for 30 minutes.
4. Remove tray from freezer, and insert a flat wooden popsicle stick into the pineapple in each divider.
5. Return tray to freezer.
6. When tray is frozen hard, each stick will hold an orange juice and pineapple pop.

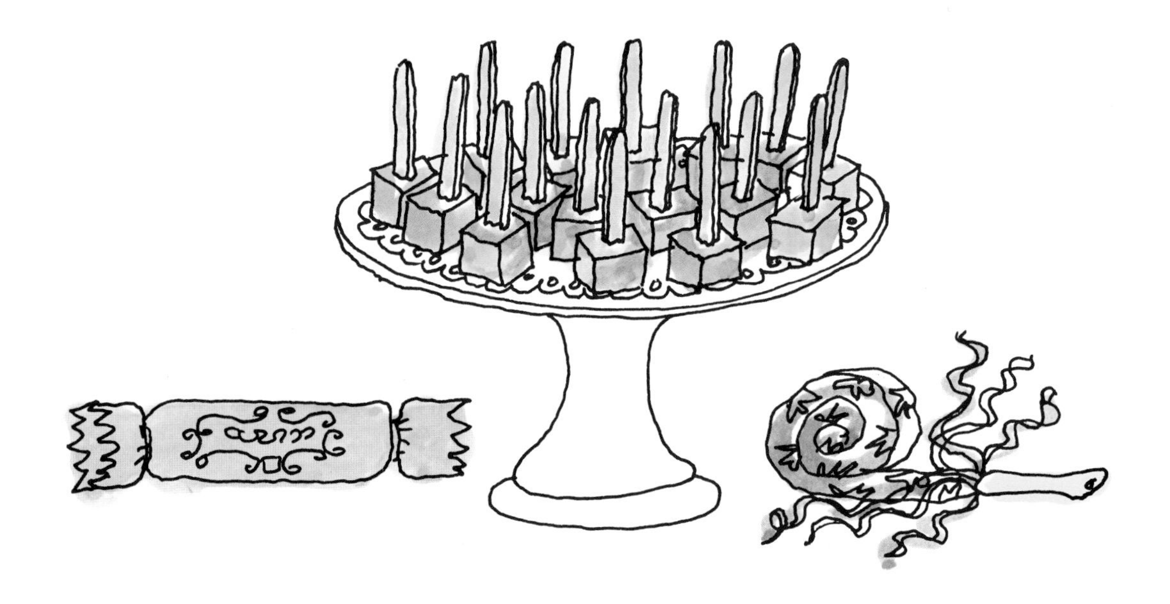

# PARTY SANDWICH BITES

YOU NEED:

8 slices of white bread
4 thick slices of ham
4 slices of American cheese
mayonnaise
1 tablespoon paprika.

WHAT YOU DO:

1. With a cookie cutter, cut out 2 circles from each slice of bread.
2. Use the cookie cutter to cut out the same shapes from the ham and cheese.
3. Spread mayonnaise on the bread circles.
4. Place ham and cheese on the bread circles.
5. Cover with another circle of bread to make a sandwich.
6. Sprinkle the tablespoon of paprika on a sheet of wax paper.
7. Run each sandwich, like a wheel, over the paprika. This will give them a nice color and flavor.

## QUICKIES

### LOUISIANA STYLE

YOU NEED:

12 toothpicks
12 tiny cooked shrimp
3 cherry tomatoes
6 gherkins (tiny pickles), cut in half

WHAT YOU DO:

1. Cut the cherry tomatoes in quarters.
2. On each toothpick, stick a gherkin, a shrimp, and a piece of tomato.

## HAWAIIAN STYLE

YOU NEED:

12 toothpicks
12 cubes of Swiss cheese
12 cubes of pineapple
12 cubes of ham

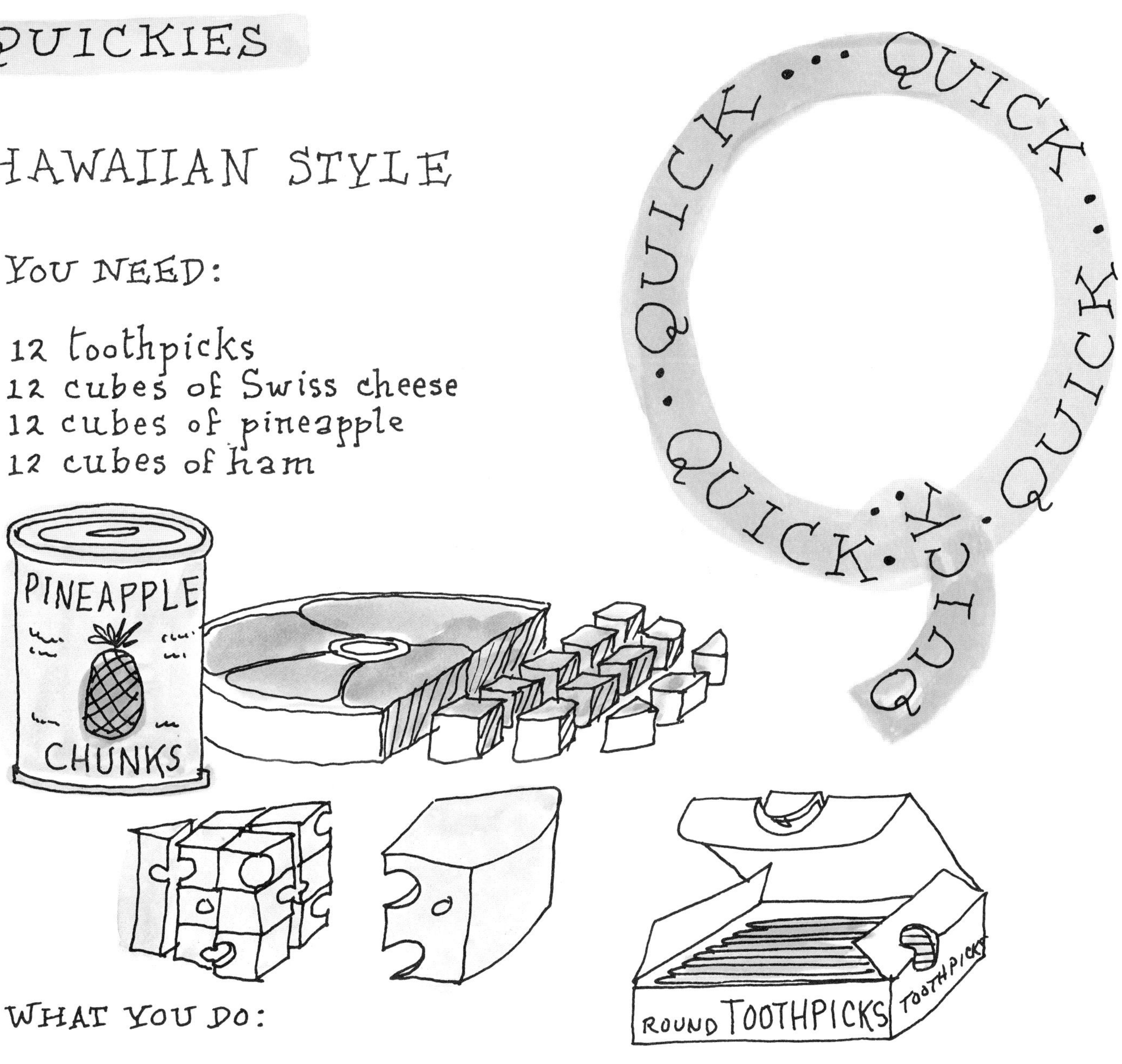


WHAT YOU DO:

1. On each toothpick, stick a piece of Swiss cheese, a piece of pineapple, and a piece of ham.

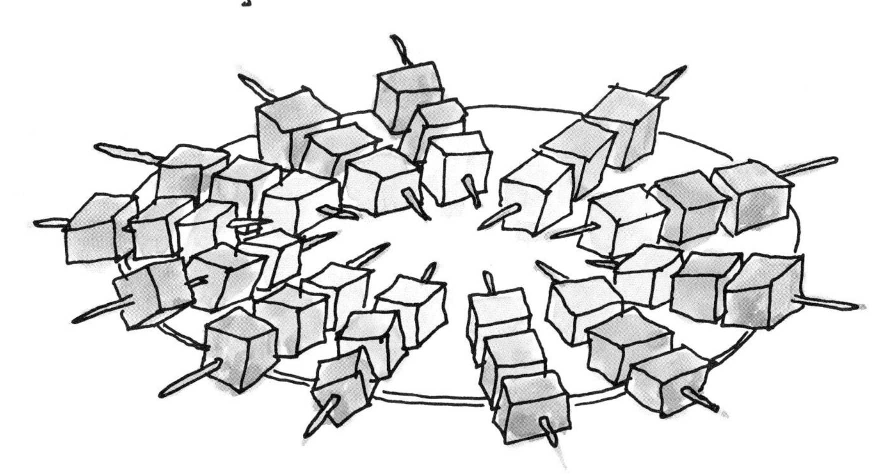

# RASPBERRY-APRICOT FREEZE

YOU NEED:

1 cup of raspberries
½ cup of apricot slices
a heaped up teaspoon of sugar
½ cup heavy cream

WHAT YOU DO:

1. Wash the raspberries.
2. Place the raspberries and apricots in a cereal bowl.
3. Add sugar.
4. In a small metal bowl, whip the cream until it is stiff.
5. Add the fruit, and mix gently.
6. Place bowl in freezer compartment of the refrigerator for 1½ hours.

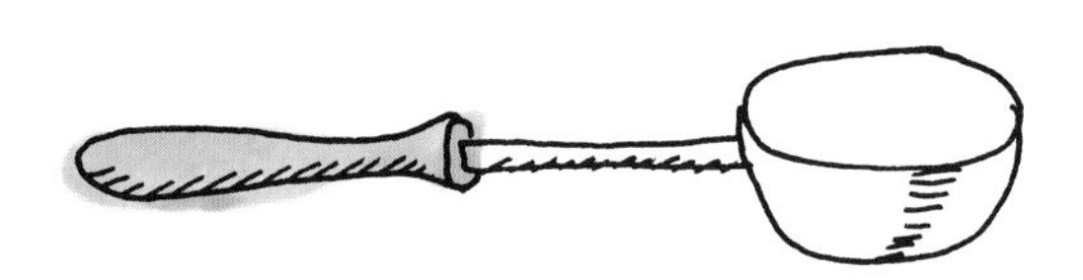

# RAISIN SALAD

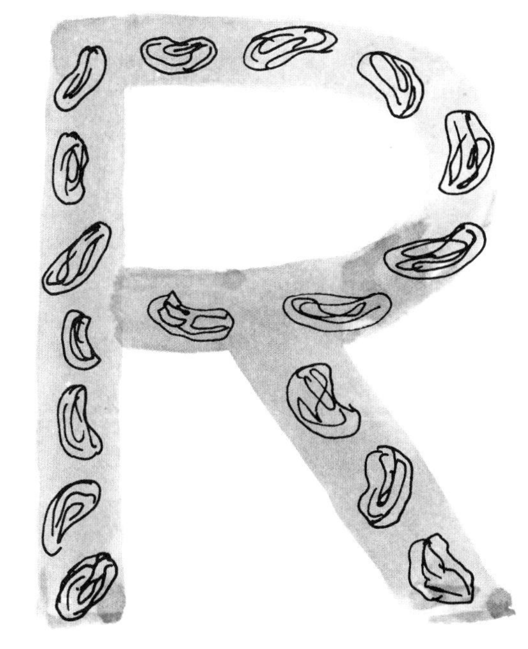

YOU NEED:

½ an apple, cut in cubes
¼ of a carrot, cut in cubes
⅓ cup of raisins
2 tablespoons mayonnaise
lettuce leaves

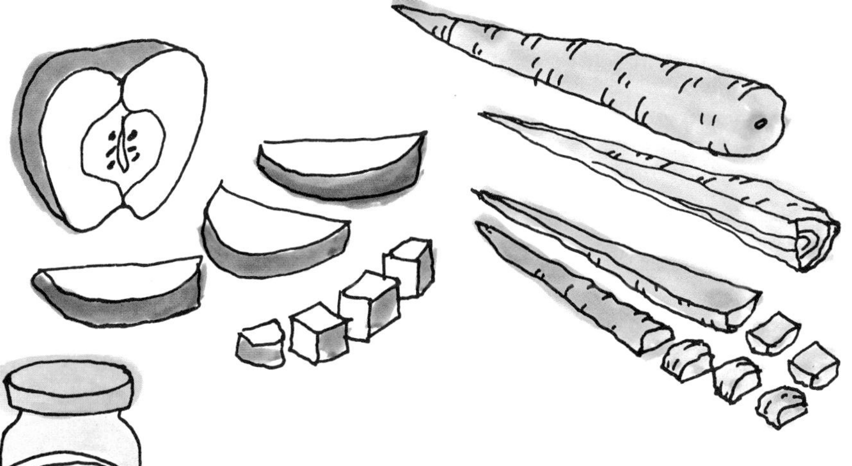

WHAT YOU DO:

1. In a cereal bowl, mix the apples, carrots, and raisins with the mayonnaise.
2. Serve on a bed of lettuce.

# SOUTHERN ICE CREAM PIE

YOU NEED:

2 cups of crushed sugar cookies
½ cup soft butter
1 pint of your favorite ice cream
3 tablespoons chopped nuts
1 slice pineapple
1 maraschino cherry

WHAT YOU DO:

1. Mix the crushed cookies with the soft butter until they form a paste.
2. Press the paste on the bottom and sides of a pie pan.
3. Put the pan in the freezer compartment of the refrigerator for 1 hour.
4. Just before you remove the pie pan from the freezer, soften the ice cream with a fork.
5. Put the nuts in the ice cream and mix.
6. When the ice cream is soft, not liquid, put it into pie pan and freeze until firm, about 1 hour. Garnish with pineapple on top of ice cream, and the cherry in the middle.

## SUNDAE, ANYDAY

YOU NEED:

1 banana
1 scoop of vanilla ice cream
1 scoop of chocolate ice cream
1 scoop of strawberry ice cream
your favorite fruit syrup
1/4 cup heavy cream
nuts

WHAT YOU DO:

1. Peel and slice a banana in half lengthwise.
2. Place the banana in a soup plate or sundae dish.
3. Place a scoop of vanilla, a scoop of chocolate, and a scoop of strawberry ice cream over banana.
4. Pour your choice of fruit syrup over the ice cream.
5. Whip the cream and put it on top.
6. Garnish with chopped nuts.

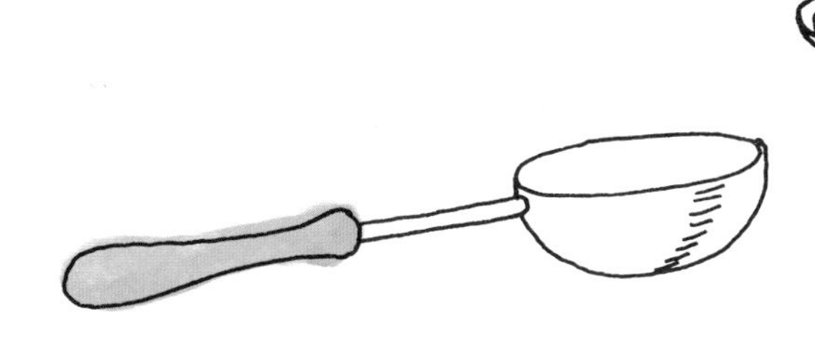

# TUNA SALAD

YOU NEED:

1 medium can of tuna fish
1 tablespoon of cut up onions
1 tablespoon of cut up celery
¼ teaspoon lemon juice
1 tablespoon mayonnaise
a little salt and pepper

WHAT YOU DO:

1. In a bowl, shred the tuna fish with a fork.
2. Add the onions and celery to the tuna and mix.
3. In a cup, mix the lemon juice and mayonnaise.
4. Add the lemon juice mixture to the tuna.
5. Mix all well together, and add a little salt and pepper.
6. Serve on top of lettuce on a plate, or as a sandwich between 2 slices of white bread.

# TOMATO SURPRISE

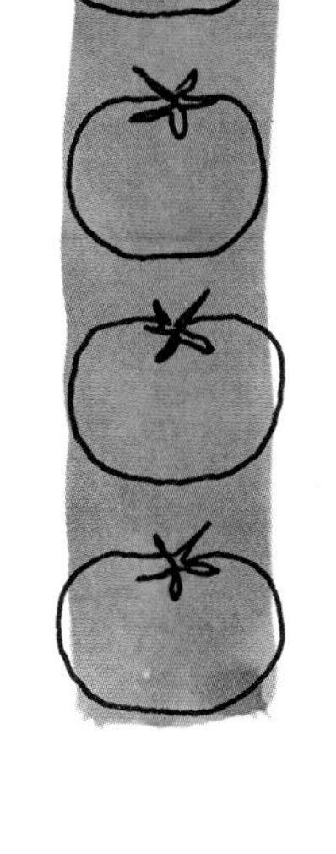

YOU NEED:

- 4 medium tomatoes
- 1 large can of mixed vegetables
- 2 tablespoons mayonnaise
- 1/4 cup of Tuna Salad (see opposite page)
- dill, cut up

WHAT YOU DO:

1. Cut off tops of tomatoes, and with a spoon, scoop out the inside of the tomatoes. (Do this very carefully so you won't break the skins.)
2. Drain the vegetables from can and put in a bowl.
3. Add the mayonnaise and mix.
4. Add a tiny bit of salt and pepper.
5. Mix in the Tuna Salad.
6. With a spoon, fill the tomatoes, and sprinkle tops with dill.

# UNCLE SAM'S RED, WHITE & BLUE FRUIT SALAD

(INSPIRED BY THE FOURTH OF JULY)

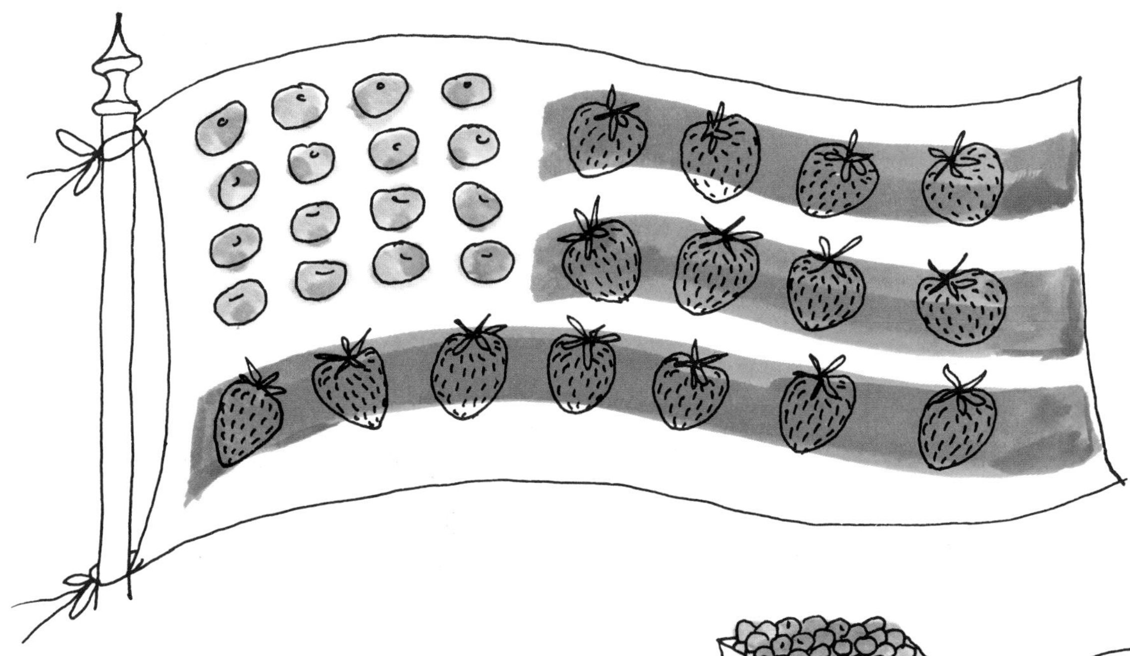

YOU NEED:

1 cup of blueberries
1 cup of strawberries, cut in half
3 tablespoons sugar
½ cup of heavy cream

WHAT YOU DO:

1. Wash the berries and put them in a cereal bowl.
2. Sprinkle sugar over the berries and mix well, but carefully.
3. Place in refrigerator to chill for 2 hours.
4. In a mixing bowl, whip the cream until it is stiff.
5. Remove berries from the refrigerator and mix with the whipped cream. Divide into 4 servings.

# URUGUAYAN SALAD

YOU NEED:

1 head of Romaine lettuce
1 large avocado, sliced
½ tablespoon lemon juice
1 tablespoon cut up onions
½ teaspoon salt
¼ teaspoon powdered mustard
¼ cup olive oil
a tiny bit of thyme

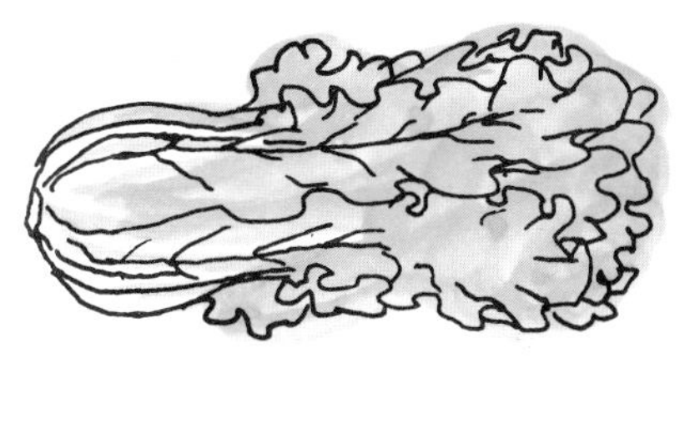

WHAT YOU DO:

1. Wash lettuce well, and break it into pieces.
2. Arrange lettuce on the bottom of a salad bowl.
3. Peel avocado, cut in half and remove stone. Cut in slices and place on top of the lettuce.
4. Sprinkle cut up onions over avocado.
5. In a cup, mix olive oil, lemon juice, powdered mustard and a little thyme.
6. Pour mixture over the salad.
7. Toss the salad and serve.

# VINAIGRETTE

YOU NEED:

3/4 cup of olive or salad oil
1/4 cup of vinegar
1 teaspoon salt
1/4 teaspoon pepper
a tiny bit of sugar
1/8 teaspoon ground rosemary

WHAT YOU DO:

1. In a cereal bowl, mix the oil with the vinegar, salt, pepper, sugar and rosemary.

This is a famous dressing used by chefs all over the world. It is good for vegetables and salads.

# V. I. P. SANDWICH

(FOR A VERY IMPORTANT PERSON)

YOU NEED:

- 2 slices of white bread, toasted if you like
- mayonnaise
- lettuce leaf
- 1 teaspoon of cut up celery
- ½ tablespoon of sliced almonds
- 3 slices of turkey
- 1 slice of tomato
- a little salt and pepper

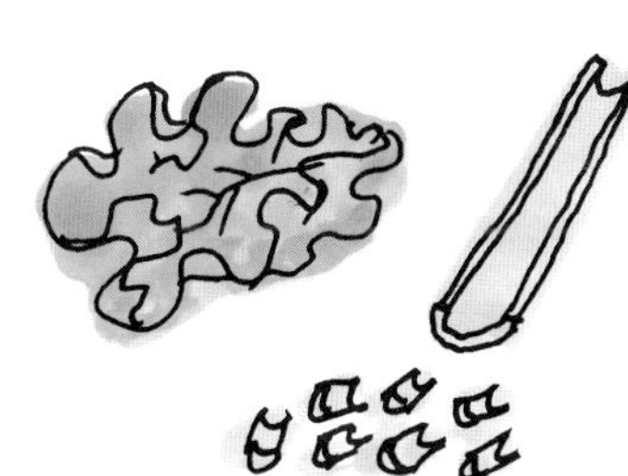

WHAT YOU DO:

1. Spread mayonnaise on both slices of bread.
2. Place a lettuce leaf on one slice of bread.
3. Place celery and almonds on lettuce.
4. Place turkey slices over lettuce, celery and almonds.
5. Top with slice of tomato.
6. Sprinkle with a little salt and pepper.
7. Cover with remaining slice of bread. Serve with a dish of applesauce.

# WALNUT WONDER

YOU NEED:

3 ounces of cream cheese
6 pitted dates, cut finely
1/4 teaspoon brown sugar
20 halves of walnuts
raisins

WHAT YOU DO:

1. Soften cream cheese with a fork.
2. Add sugar and dates to the cream cheese.
3. With a butter knife, spread the mixture thickly on half a walnut.
4. Cover this with another walnut half to make a nut sandwich.
5. Stick raisins in on the sides of the nut sandwich where the cream cheese shows.

# WALDORF SALAD

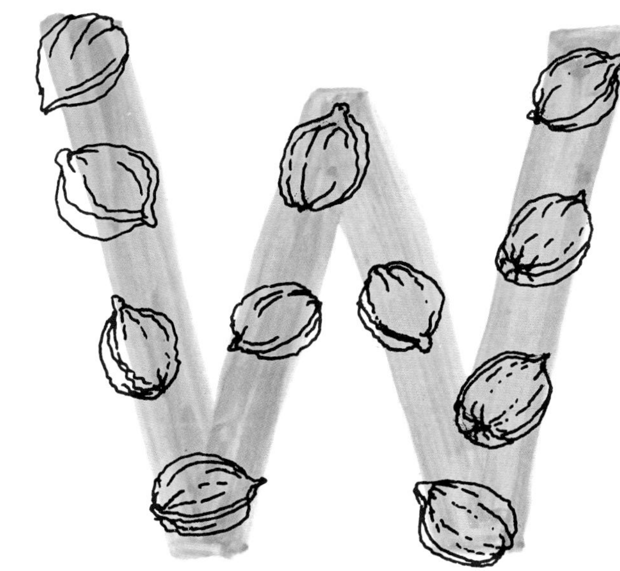

YOU NEED:

- lettuce leaves
- ¾ cup diced celery
- 1 cup peeled, cored, diced apples
- 5 tablespoons of walnuts cut in small pieces
- ½ cup mayonnaise

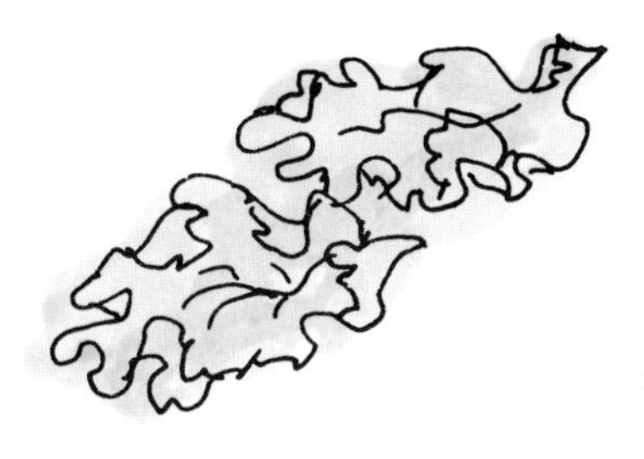

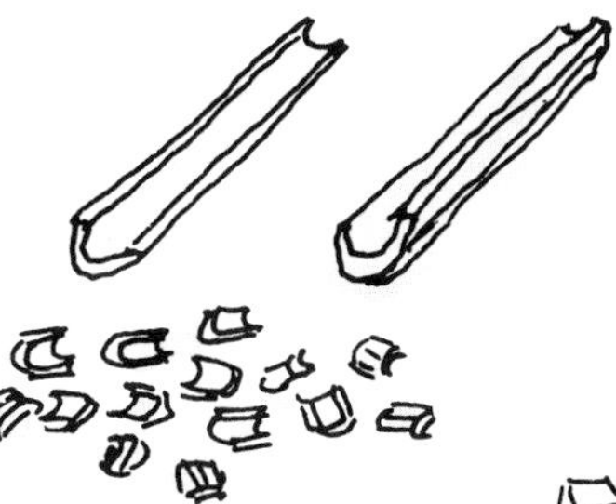

WHAT YOU DO:

1. Wash and dry the lettuce leaves.
2. Line a salad bowl with the lettuce leaves.
3. In a cereal bowl, mix together the celery, apples, walnuts and mayonnaise.
4. Place the vegetable, fruit and nuts mixture on a bed of lettuce.

The Waldorf Salad is internationally known.

# XYLOPHONE DIPS

## BLUE DANUBE DIP

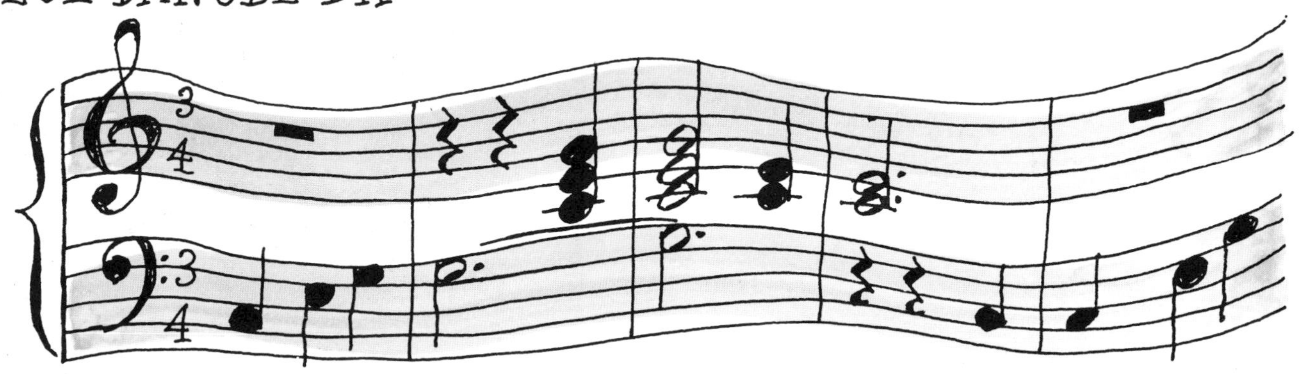

YOU NEED:

1 tablespoon Blue cheese
1 medium onion, cut in little pieces
1/4 cup mayonnaise
3/4 cup sour cream
1/2 teaspoon freshly ground pepper

WHAT YOU DO:

1. In a mixing bowl, mash the cheese with a fork.
2. Mix cheese with sour cream and mayonnaise.
3. Add the cut up onions and the pepper.
4. Mix well.

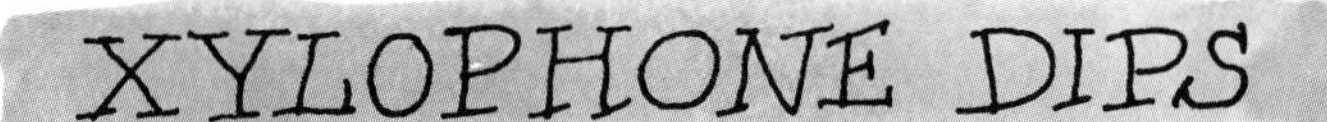


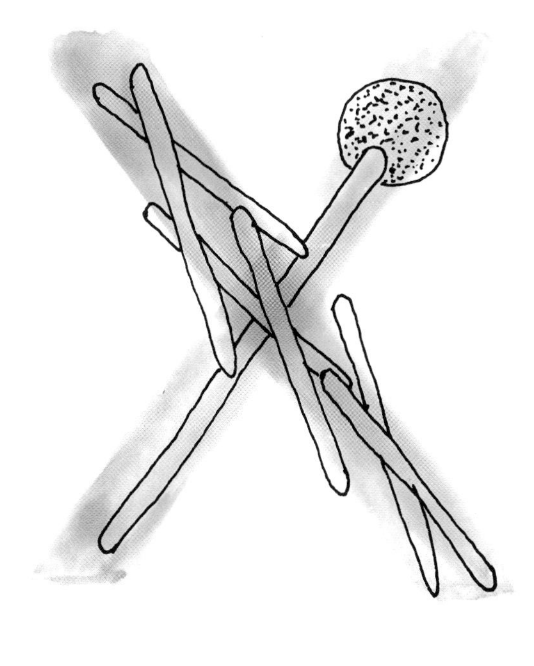

YOU NEED:

3 ounces of cream cheese
2 tablespoons mayonnaise
1 garlic clove, crushed
1 tablespoon of onion pieces
a little salt and pepper

WHAT YOU DO:

1. Soften the cream cheese with a fork.
2. Add mayonnaise to cheese and mix.
3. Add garlic, onions and a little salt and pepper.
4. Mix well.

The names for the Xylophone Dips were inspired by the tasty *thin* Italian breadsticks which resemble the thin sticks used to play the xylophone. We use the breadsticks to enjoy the "musical" dips.

# YOGHURT AND CUCUMBER SALAD

YOU NEED:

2 cucumbers
1/4 cup fresh mint, cut finely
1/4 cup fresh parsley, cut finely
1 cup plain yoghurt
1/4 teaspoon salt
1/8 teaspoon pepper
1/4 teaspoon lemon juice

WHAT YOU DO:

1. Peel cucumbers and slice thinly.
2. Place cucumbers in a mixing bowl with mint and parsley.
3. Add yoghurt, salt, pepper and lemon juice. Mix all well together.
4. Place in the refrigerator to chill until you are ready to serve it.

# YOGHURT AND FRUIT

YOU NEED:

1 cup plain yoghurt
3 fresh peaches, washed, peeled, and sliced, or a small can of sliced peaches
1 teaspoon honey

WHAT YOU DO:

1. In a mixing bowl, mix the peaches with honey and yoghurt.
2. Keep in the refrigerator until you are ready to serve it.

# ZIPPY SALAMI BITS

YOU NEED:

6 soda crackers
cream cheese
6 slices of salami
1 teaspoon parsley, finely cut

WHAT YOU DO:

1. Spread cream cheese on the crackers.
2. Sprinkle a bit of parsley on the cheese.
3. Put a slice of salami on each cracker.

# ZODIAC TREATS

YOU NEED:

4 slices of white bread, or more
peanut butter
orange marmalade
grape jelly
strawberry jelly

WHAT YOU DO:

1. With cookie cutters, cut out suns, moons and stars from the slices of bread.
2. Spread peanut butter on all of the shapes.
3. Put orange marmalade on the round or sun shapes.
4. Spread grape jelly on the crescent or moon shapes.
5. Spread strawberry jelly on the star shapes.

THE END

All good cooks have their own favorite recipes . . .
Use these pages to write down <u>your</u> own recipes.

# RECIPES

# RECIPES

# RECIPES

# RECIPES

# RECIPES

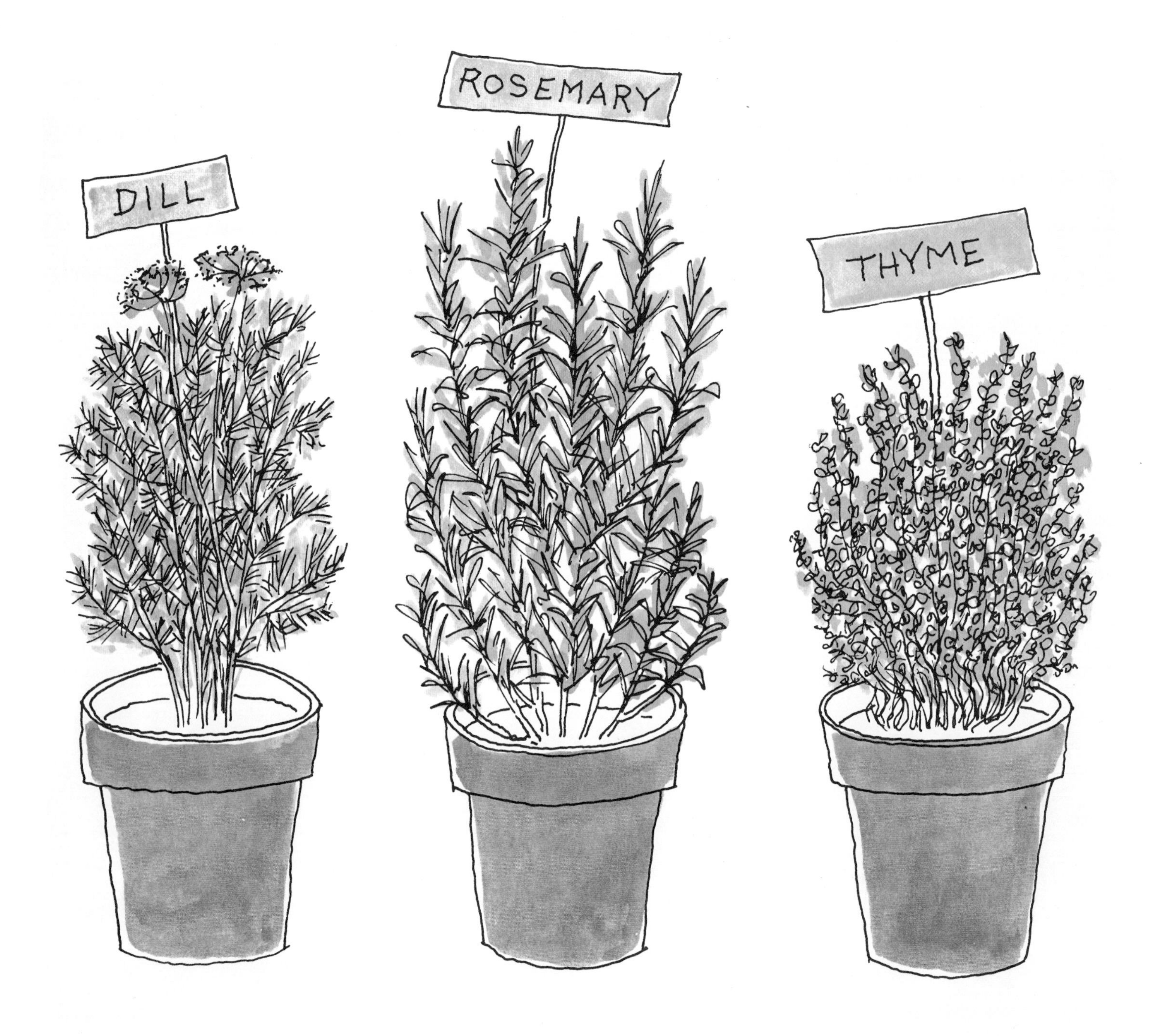
DILL
ROSEMARY
THYME